RECORD BREAKERS

BASEBALL

Blaine Wiseman

MEDIA ENHANCED BOOKS
AV2 BY WEIGL
ADDED VALUE · AUDIO VISUAL

www.av2books.com

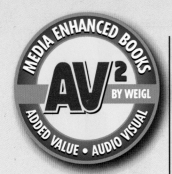

AV² **by Weigl** brings you media enhanced books that support active learning.

AV² provides enriched content that supplements and complements this book. Weigl's AV² books strive to create inspired learning and engage young minds for a total learning experience.

Go to **www.av2books.com**, and enter this book's unique code. You will have access to video, audio, web links, quizzes, a slide show, and activities.

BOOK CODE

Y 1 0 8 9 8 0

Audio
Listen to sections of the book read aloud.

Video
Watch informative video clips.

Web Link
Find research sites and play interactive games.

Try This!
Complete activities and hands-on experiments.

Due to the dynamic nature of the Internet, some of the URLs and activities provided as part of AV² by Weigl may have changed or ceased to exist. AV² by Weigl accepts no responsibility for any such changes. All media enhanced books are regularly monitored to update addresses and sites in a timely manner. Contact AV² by Weigl at 1-866-649-3445 or av2books@weigl.com with any questions, comments, or feedback.

Published by AV² by Weigl
350 5th Avenue, 59th Floor
New York, NY 10118
Website: www.av2books.com   www.weigl.com

Library of Congress Cataloging-in-Publication Data available upon request.
Fax 1-866-44-WEIGL for the attention of the Publishing Records department.

ISBN 978-1-61690-109-7 (hard cover)
ISBN 978-1-61690-110-3 (soft cover)

Printed in the United States of America in North Mankato, Minnesota
1 2 3 4 5 6 7 8 9 0 14 13 12 11 10

052010
WEP264000

Project Coordinator Heather C. Hudak
Design Terry Paulhus

Photo Credits
Every reasonable effort has been made to trace ownership and to obtain permission to reprint copyright material. The publishers would be pleased to have any errors or omissions brought to their attention so that they may be corrected in subsequent printings.

Weigl acknowledges Getty Images as its primary image supplier for this title.

Contents

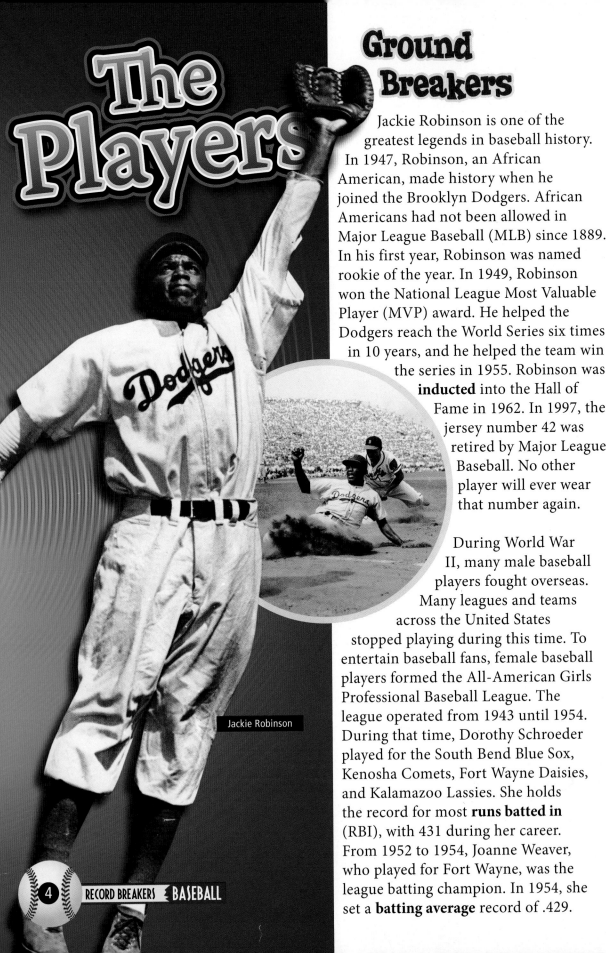

The Players

Ground Breakers

Jackie Robinson is one of the greatest legends in baseball history. In 1947, Robinson, an African American, made history when he joined the Brooklyn Dodgers. African Americans had not been allowed in Major League Baseball (MLB) since 1889. In his first year, Robinson was named rookie of the year. In 1949, Robinson won the National League Most Valuable Player (MVP) award. He helped the Dodgers reach the World Series six times in 10 years, and he helped the team win the series in 1955. Robinson was **inducted** into the Hall of Fame in 1962. In 1997, the jersey number 42 was retired by Major League Baseball. No other player will ever wear that number again.

During World War II, many male baseball players fought overseas. Many leagues and teams across the United States stopped playing during this time. To entertain baseball fans, female baseball players formed the All-American Girls Professional Baseball League. The league operated from 1943 until 1954. During that time, Dorothy Schroeder played for the South Bend Blue Sox, Kenosha Comets, Fort Wayne Daisies, and Kalamazoo Lassies. She holds the record for most **runs batted in** (RBI), with 431 during her career. From 1952 to 1954, Joanne Weaver, who played for Fort Wayne, was the league batting champion. In 1954, she set a **batting average** record of .429.

Jackie Robinson

Home Run Hitters

Although it lasts only a second or two, a home run is one of the most exciting plays in baseball. In his 23 seasons playing for such teams as the Milwaukee Braves, Atlanta Braves, and Milwaukee Brewers, Hammerin' Hank Aaron knocked the ball over the fence 755 times.

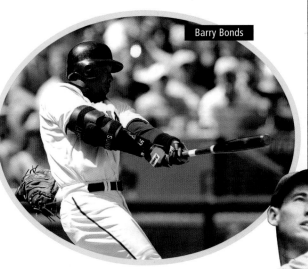
Barry Bonds

Home Records Hitters

Barry Bonds – 768
Pittsburgh Pirates, San Francisco Giants

Hank Aaron – 755
Milwaukee/Atlanta Braves, Milwaukee Brewers

Babe Ruth – 714
Boston Red Sox, New York Yankees, Boston Braves

Willie Mays – 660
New York/San Francisco Giants, New York Mets

Ken Griffey, Jr. – 630
Seattle Mariners, Cincinnati Reds, Chicago White Sox

Barry Bonds broke Aaron's record in 2007. However, Bonds used performance enhancing drugs, such as steroids. Steroids add strength to muscles, but cause health issues, including heart problems. For this reason, many people still consider Aaron the home run king.

Season Hitters

Only five baseball players have hit 60 or more home runs in one year. Mark McGwire and Sammy Sosa have achieved this feat more than once. Both players have also been connected to steroid use.

Player	Home Runs in One Season	Year
Barry Bonds	73	2001
Mark McGwire	70	1998
Sammy Sosa	66	1998
Mark McGwire	65	1999
Sammy Sosa	64	2001
Sammy Sosa	63	1999
Roger Maris	61	1961
Babe Ruth	60	1927

★ BEST AT BAT ★

Known as "Teddy Ballgame" and "Terrible Ted," Ted Williams is thought to be the greatest hitter of all time. In 1941, he batted .406, meaning he made a hit more than 40 percent of the times he batted. No player has broken .400 since Williams achieved this feat. Over his career, Williams' batting average was .344.

The Fielders

Smarter Than Your Average Catcher

Yogi Berra is one of the greatest back catchers in baseball history. However, he is better known for his memorable quotes. During his career with the New York Yankees, Berra won 10 World Series championships. This is more than any other player. Berra caught the only **perfect game** in World Series history and hit the first **pinch hit** home run in the World Series. Here are some well-known quotes from Berra.

Making a Pitch

Baseball is a team game, so pitchers are judged more by wins than by any other statistic. To win a game, a pitcher must use many different pitches and strategies to beat batters. These pitchers won more games than any other pitcher in history.

Pitcher	Wins
Cy Young Cleveland Spiders, St. Louis Perfectos/Cardinals, Boston Americans/Red Sox, Cleveland Naps, Boston Rustlers	511
Walter Johnson Washington Senators	417
Grover Alexander Philadelphia Phillies, Chicago Cubs, St. Louis Cardinals	373
Christy Mathewson New York Giants, Cincinnati Reds	373
Warren Spahn Boston/Milwaukee Braves, New York Mets, San Francisco Giants	363

"IT AIN'T OVER 'TIL IT'S OVER."

"YOU CAN OBSERVE A LOT BY WATCHING."

"THE FUTURE AIN'T WHAT IT USED TO BE."

"I DIDN'T REALLY SAY EVERYTHING I SAID."

Warren Spahn

Yogi Berra

Randy Johnson

Three Strikes

The best way for a pitcher to put a batter out is with a **strike out**. These are the strike out kings of the Major Leagues.

Strike Out Kings

Nolan Ryan – 5,714
New York Mets, California Angels, Houston Astros, Texas Rangers

Randy Johnson – 4,875
Montreal Expos, Seattle Mariners, Houston Astros, Arizona Diamondbacks, New York Yankees, San Francisco Giants

Roger Clemons – 4,672
Boston Red Sox, Toronto Blue Jays, New York Yankees, Houston Astros

Steve Carlton – 4,136
St. Louis Cardinals, Philadelphia Phillies, San Francisco Giants, Chicago White Sox, Cleveland Indians, Minnesota Twins

Bert Blyleven – 3,701
Minnesota Twins, Texas Rangers, Pittsburgh Pirates, Cleveland Indians, Minnesota Twins, California Angels

Joel Zumaya

Pitcher	Speed (mph)	Year
Joel Zumaya	104.8	2006
Mark Wohlers	103	1995
Armando Benitez	102	2002
Jonathan Broxton	102	2009
Bobby Jenks	102	2005
Randy Johnson	102	2004
Matt Lindstrom	102	2007
Rob Nenn	102	1997
Justin Verlander	102	2007

Throwing Smoke

Nolan Ryan is known as the fastest pitcher in baseball. This strike out king used his blazing pitching speed to beat batters. Although others have thrown pitches faster than Ryan, he threw consistently at about 100 miles per hour (161 kilometers per hour) for his entire career. This list shows the pitchers with the fastest pitches through history.

Nolan Ryan

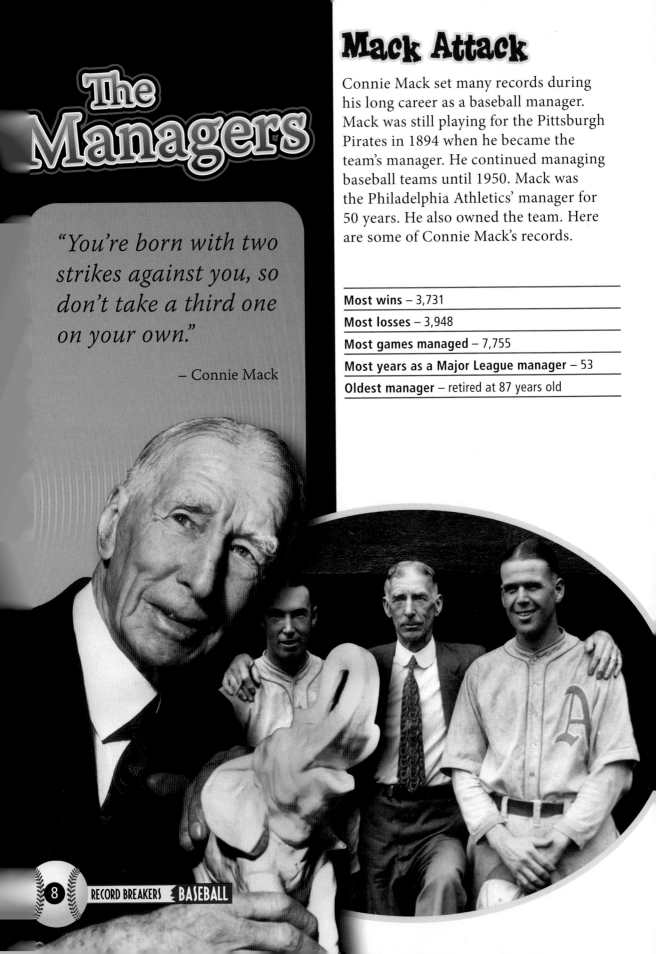

The Managers

"You're born with two strikes against you, so don't take a third one on your own."

– Connie Mack

Mack Attack

Connie Mack set many records during his long career as a baseball manager. Mack was still playing for the Pittsburgh Pirates in 1894 when he became the team's manager. He continued managing baseball teams until 1950. Mack was the Philadelphia Athletics' manager for 50 years. He also owned the team. Here are some of Connie Mack's records.

Most wins – 3,731	
Most losses – 3,948	
Most games managed – 7,755	
Most years as a Major League manager – 53	
Oldest manager – retired at 87 years old	

Leading the Charge

These managers have led their teams to the most World Series championships.

Mickey Mantle and Casey Stengel

World Series Managers	Wins
Casey Stengel New York Yankees 1949–1953, 1956, 1958	7
Joe McCarthy New York Yankees 1932,1936–1939, 1941, 1943	7
Connie Mack Philadelphia Athletics 1910, 1911, 1913, 1929, 1930	5
Walter Alston Los Angeles Dodgers 1955, 1959, 1963, 1965	4
Joe Torre New York Yankees 1996, 1998–2000	4

Joe Torre

You're Outta Here!

Baseball managers are known for throwing outrageous temper tantrums and having heated arguments with umpires. The umpire can choose to **eject** the manager from the game. These are the most ejected managers.

Bobby Cox

Manager	Ejections in Career
Bobby Cox Atlanta Braves	143
John McGraw Baltimore Orioles, New York Giants	117
Earl Weaver Baltimore Orioles	97
Leo Durocher Brooklyn Dodgers, New York Giants, Chicago Cubs, Houston Astros	95
Frankie Frisch St. Louis Cardinals, Pittsburgh Pirates, Chicago Cubs	82

The World Series

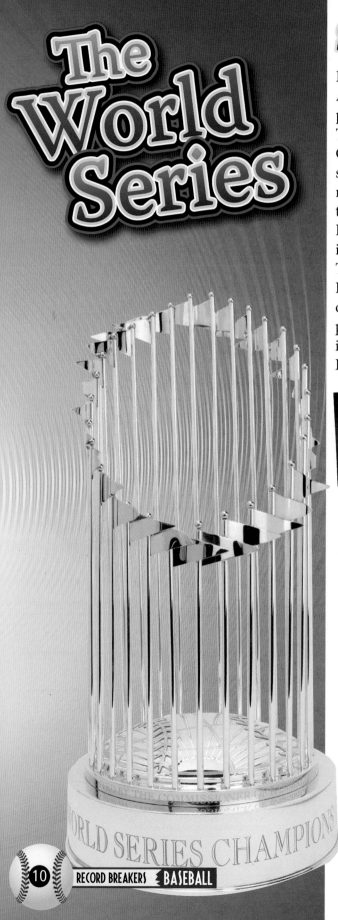

Sizing It Up

Each year, the champions of the American and National Leagues meet to play for the World Series championship. The winner of the series is awarded the Commissioner's Trophy. This **sterling** silver award has 30 gold-plated flags rising above a baseball, which represents the world. The flags represent each Major League team. Each year, a new trophy is made by Tiffany & Co. in New York. This process takes about three months. It stands 24 inches (61 centimeters) tall on top of a base and weighs about 30 pounds (14 kilograms). The trophy's base is signed by the commissioner of Major League Baseball.

★ WORLD SERIES RECORDS ★

Mickey Mantle – Home runs (18)
New York Yankees

Whitey Ford – Games won (10)
New York Yankees

Whitey Ford – Strikeouts (94)
New York Yankees

Mariano Rivera – Saves (11)
New York Yankees

Yogi Berra – Hits (71)
New York Yankees

Pepper Martin – Batting Average (.418)
St. Louis Cardinals

Paul Molitor – Batting Average (.418)
Toronto Blue Jays

Billy Goat's Grudge

In 1945, the Chicago Cubs were in the midst of a long championship **drought** when a man and his goat put a curse on the team. The man owned a local bar, called the "Billy Goat Tavern." He brought his pet goat, Murphy, to game four of the World Series. Near the end of the game, the man and his goat were thrown out of the park because his goat's odor was bothering fans. As he was leaving the ballpark, the man said, "The Cubs will never win another World Series until the goat is allowed in Wrigley Field." After the Cubs lost game seven of the series, the goat's owner sent a letter to the Cubs' owner. The letter said, "Who stinks now?" Goats still are not allowed in Wrigley Field, and the Cubs still have not won a World Series since 1908.

Who Stinks now?

Babe Ruth

The Curse of the Bambino

The most important deal in baseball history happened between the Boston Red Sox and New York Yankees in 1920. The Red Sox were the most successful Major League Baseball team. They had won their fifth World Series two years earlier. The Yankees paid Boston $125,000 for a young pitcher named George Herman "Babe" Ruth. "The Great Bambino" became the greatest legend in baseball. He helped turn the Yankees into a baseball dynasty. The Red Sox did not win another championship until 2004. The 86-year gap between their championship wins is blamed on "The Curse of the Bambino."

Trophy Collectors

The New York Yankees are the most successful team in professional sports. They have played in 40 World Series. In 2009, the Yankees won their 27th title, beating the Philadelphia Phillies in six games. In 1903, the Boston Americans, who later became known as the Red Sox, won the first World Series by beating the Pittsburgh Pirates. Here are the teams that have won the most championships.

New York Yankees	27	Boston Red Sox/Americans	7
St. Louis Cardinals	10	Los Angeles/Brooklyn Dodgers	6
Oakland/Philadelphia Athletics	9		

The Gear

Uniforms

Every baseball team has its own uniform. The uniform has a unique logo and colors. The first baseball uniform was worn by the New York Knickerbockers in 1849. In the 19th century, some uniforms included straw hats and bow ties. In 1881, a new rule stated that each player had to wear a colored shirt with white pants. The color of the shirt represented the player's position. Pitchers wore light blue, while left fielders wore white. Second basemen wore orange with black stripes. Players found the rule confusing, and it was changed mid-season.

The Ball

The type of baseball used today has been made the same way since 1872. Before this, balls were made by wrapping string or yarn around a solid core. The core could be made of any material. A piece of brown leather was stitched together to make a cover. These balls were very light. Today's baseballs are made of wool yarn wrapped around a vulcanized rubber core. The cover consists of two pieces of white leather that are stitched together in a figure eight pattern. These balls weigh between 5 and 5.25 ounces (142 and 149 grams).

Bats

Early baseball bats were very similar in size and shape to today's bats. However, they were thicker and heavier. In MLB, bats are made out of wood. Hickory, ash, and maple are the most popular types of wood used to make bats. Some players have been caught putting cork inside their bats. This makes the bat lighter, allowing the player to swing it faster. Putting cork inside the bat is not allowed. Sammy Sosa was caught using a corked bat in 2003. He was suspended for seven games.

Gloves

The first baseball players did not wear gloves. Balls were lighter than they are today, so players used their bare hands to catch them. The first players to wear gloves were catchers and first basemen. Players in these positions catch the most balls during a game. At first, players wore leather work gloves without full fingers. As baseballs became harder and heavier, padding was added to the gloves, and the fingers were extended to make a basket. Bid McPhee, of the Cincinnati Reds, was the last MLB player to not use a glove. He began wearing a glove in 1895.

More Records

To Catch a Thief

In baseball, stealing a base is an exciting play that helps the team. Stealing is when a player runs from one base to the next while a pitch is being thrown. These players made a career out of stealing.

Player	Stolen Bases
Rickey Henderson	1,406
Lou Brock	938
Billy Hamilton	912
Ty Cobb	892
Tim Raines	808

Rickey Henderson

Into the Sunset

Mickey Mantle

A walk off home run is when a player ends a game with one swing of the bat, and then walks off the field. Mickey Mantle is the greatest walk off home run hitter of all time. In total, he ended 13 games with home runs. In the 1964 World Series, Mantle hit a solo home run to win game three against the St. Louis Cardinals. Every ballplayer dreams of winning the World Series with a walk off home run. Only Bill Mazeroski and Joe Carter have ever achieved this dream. They won the World Series with one swing of their bat.

David Ortiz, of the Boston Red Sox, has hit 12 walk off home runs during his career. His best-known walk off home run beat the Yankees in game four of the 2004 American League Championship Series (ALCS). The hit saved the Sox's season, and the team went on to win eight games in a row for the World Series title.

Iron Horses

In a 162-game season, it is common for ballplayers to become injured. Teams sometimes play two games in one day, and the travel schedule can be exhausting. Players who have long streaks of not missing a game are respected in the MLB for their perseverance and ability to avoid injuries. Lou Gehrig played his first Major League game for the Yankees in 1925. He played his last game 13 years later. "The Iron Horse" did not miss a single game during that time.

In total, Gehrig played 2,130 games in a row. He played with a broken thumb, broken toe, and a sore back. Gehrig's hand was fractured 17 times in his career. He never went to the doctor, and the fractures healed on their own. Gehrig always played through the pain. On May 2, 1939, health problems ended Gehrig's streak. He died two years later from a disease called ALS, which is now known as Lou Gehrig's disease.

Gehrig's record stood until 1995, when Cal Ripken Jr. of the Baltimore Orioles played in his 2,131st straight game. Ripken, one of the greatest players of his time, played a total of 2,632 games in a row.

Lou Gehrig

World Series Most Valuable Players

While baseball is a team sport, outstanding individual performances can be the difference in winning a championship. In Major League Baseball, the player who is the most important to his team winning the World Series is named World Series Most Valuable Player (**MVP**). Here are the last six players to receive that award.

NORTH AMERICA

SOUTH AMERICA

Jermaine Dye

MVP 2005

Born: Vacaville, California
Position: Outfielder
Team: Chicago White Sox

Cole Hamels

MVP 2008

Born: San Diego, California
Position: Starting Pitcher
Team: Philadelphia Phillies

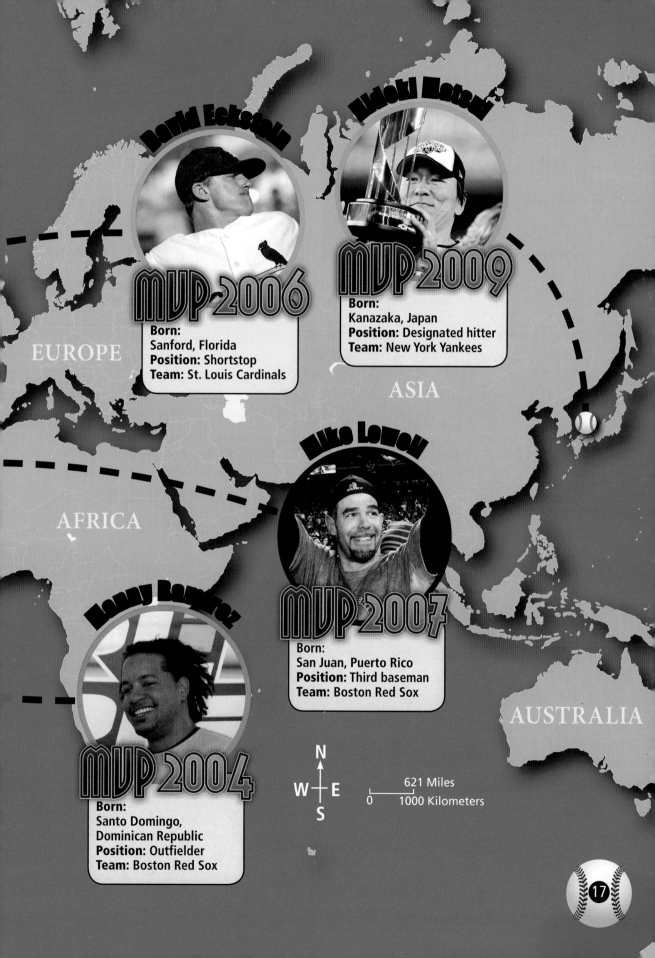

David Eckstein

MVP 2006

Born:
Sanford, Florida
Position: Shortstop
Team: St. Louis Cardinals

Hideki Matsui

MVP 2009

Born:
Kanazaka, Japan
Position: Designated hitter
Team: New York Yankees

EUROPE

ASIA

Mike Lowell

MVP 2007

Born:
San Juan, Puerto Rico
Position: Third baseman
Team: Boston Red Sox

AFRICA

AUSTRALIA

Manny Ramirez

MVP 2004

Born:
Santo Domingo,
Dominican Republic
Position: Outfielder
Team: Boston Red Sox

N
W E
S

621 Miles
0   1000 Kilometers

The Ballpark

The Originals

The first stadium ever built for baseball was Philadelphia's Shibe Park. Built in 1909, the park was home to the Philadelphia Athletics. It could seat up to 20,000 fans. After the Athletics left, the Phillies moved in. The Phillies played there until 1970. When the team moved to Veterans' Stadium, the home plate from Shibe was brought to the new stadium.

The oldest ballpark still used in MLB is Boston's Fenway Park. This ballpark hosted its first game in 1912. The park is known for its odd shape, with corners in the center field wall, as well as a huge left field wall called "the Green Monster." The Green Monster stands 37 feet tall and has seats at the top where fans can enjoy a unique view of Major League ball games.

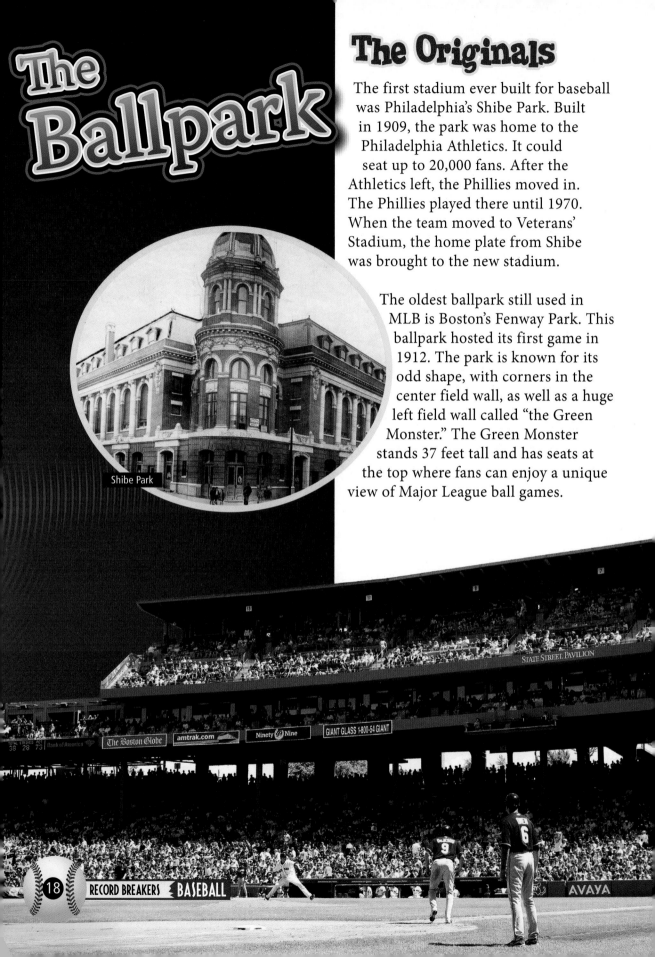

Shibe Park

STATE STREET PAVILION

TOTAL STRIKES PCT
36 28 73 Bank of America   The Boston Globe   amtrak.com   Ninety Nine   GIANT GLASS 1-800-54 GIANT

AVAYA

Costly Construction

The new Yankee Stadium was a huge construction project. It took almost three years to complete. The new stadium was built across the street from the original Yankee Stadium, and the front of the building was made to look the same as the original. The building contains a hotel and a high school. The project cost a total of $1.5 billion.

The Biggest Barns

In 2009, the greatest team in baseball history played its first game at a new stadium. The new Yankee Stadium in New York replaced the old one, becoming the second-biggest stadium in MLB. These are the biggest stadiums in baseball.

Stadium	Team	Seats
Dodger Stadium	Los Angeles Dodgers	56,000
Yankee Stadium	New York Yankees	52,325
Rogers Centre	Toronto Blue Jays	50,516
Coors Field	Colorado Rockies	50,445
Turner Field	Atlanta Braves	50,096

In 1976, Montreal, Canada, hosted the Summer Olympics. A new stadium was built for the games. Olympic Stadium, or "the Big O," later became the home of the Montreal Expos. Organizers expected the project to cost about $100 million dollars. By the time construction costs were completely paid in 2006, the stadium had cost $1.5 billion. The Big O has also been called "the Big Owe" and "the Big Mistake" because of how much money was owed for its construction.

In The Money

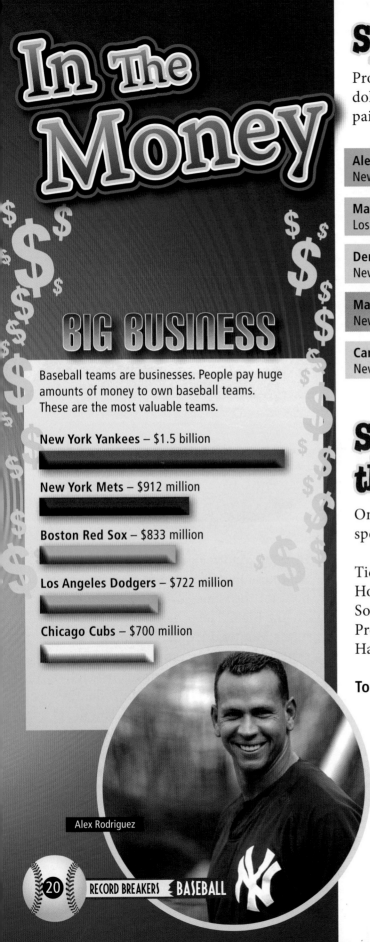

BIG BUSINESS

Baseball teams are businesses. People pay huge amounts of money to own baseball teams. These are the most valuable teams.

New York Yankees – $1.5 billion

New York Mets – $912 million

Boston Red Sox – $833 million

Los Angeles Dodgers – $722 million

Chicago Cubs – $700 million

Alex Rodriguez

Sporting Salaries

Professional baseball players earn top dollar. Annually, these athletes are paid the most money in their sport.

Alex Rodriguez – $33 million
New York Yankees

Manny Ramirez – $23.9 million
Los Angeles Dodgers

Derek Jeter – $21.6 million
New York Yankees

Mark Teixeira – $20.6 million
New York Yankees

Carlos Beltran – $19.2 million
New York Mets

Spending at the Game

On average, how much do people spend at a baseball game?

Ticket: $26.75
Hot dog: $3.75
Soft drink: $3.50
Program: $3.75
Hat: $15

Total: $52.75

Culture

Ballpark tradition

Americans have played and watched baseball for more than 100 years, and many traditions have formed. The 27th U.S. president, William Howard Taft, started two of these traditions. At the first game of the 1910 season, between the Philadelphia Athletics and the Washington Senators, the umpire handed the ball to the president and asked him to throw it over home plate. Since 1910, every president has thrown out the opening pitch of a baseball season. Jimmy Carter in the only president to wait until he was out of office to participate in the tradition.

President William Howard Taft

Mr. Met

Biggest Fans

Mascots perform stunts and excite crowds with their wild antics. The first Major League Baseball mascot was Mr. Met. Mr. Met began cheering for the New York Mets in 1964. His huge, baseball head, topped with a Mets cap, can be seen rallying the crowd at Citi Field during every Mets game. The 6-foot 6-inch (198-cm) tall, green-feathered Phanatic, another mascot, has been cheering on the Phillies since 1978. Today, almost every Major League team has a mascot that helps get fans excited.

Collector's Items

Baseball cards were created in the 1800s and have become a popular collector's item with millions of fans around the world. The first cards were made to promote products such as baseball equipment. Over time, chewing gum companies began to include cards in gum packs. Today, baseball cards are sold in sets or in packs of a few cards.

QUIZ

1 Who was the first African American to play Major League Baseball?

2 Who was the last player to bat better than 400 in a season?

3 What pitcher struck out more batters than any other pitcher?

4 What record does Bobby Cox hold?

5 What caused the "Curse of the Bambino"?

6 Who was the last fielder to play barehanded?

7 Name the only two players to win the World Series with walk off home runs.

8 What is the oldest stadium still used in the MLB?

9 Who is the highest paid player in the MLB?

10 Who was the first president to throw the opening day pitch?

ANSWERS: 1. Jackie Robinson 2. Ted Williams 3. Nolan Ryan 4. Most ejections 5. The sale of Babe Ruth from the Red Sox to the Yankees 6. Bid McPhee 7. Bill Mazeroski and Joe Carter 8. Fenway Park 9. Alex Rodriguez 10. President William Howard Taft

GLOSSARY

batting average: a number that represents a player's hits compared to outs; 1.000 equals 100 percent

drought: a long period without success

eject: throw out of a game

inducted: formally admitted

MVP: most valuable player

perfect game: a game in which the pitcher does not allow any player from the other team to reach base

pinch hit: when a player replaces another player to bat

runs batted in: when a player gets a hit that gets one of his or her teammates to home plate

sterling: made of fine-quality silver

strike out: when a batter gets three strikes against him or her while at-bat

INDEX

Log on to www.av2books.com

AV² by Weigl brings you media enhanced books that support active learning. Go to **www.av2books.com**, and enter the special code inside the front cover of this book. You will gain access to enriched and enhanced content that supplements and complements this book. Content includes video, audio, web links, quizzes, a slide show, and activities.

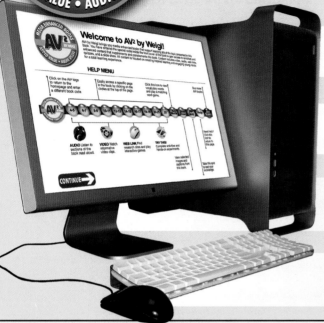

Audio
Listen to sections of the book read aloud.

Video
Watch informative video clips.

Web Link
Find research sites and play interactive games.

Try This!
Complete activities and hands-on experiments.

WHAT'S ONLINE?

Try This! Complete activities and hands-on experiments.	**Web Link** Find research sites and play interactive games.	**Video** Watch informative video clips.	**EXTRA FEATURES**
Pages 10-11 Try this baseball activity.	**Pages 6-7** Learn more about baseball players.	**Pages 4-5** Watch a video about baseball.	**Audio** Hear introductory audio at the top of every page
Pages 12-13 Test your knowledge of baseball gear.	**Pages 8-9** Read about baseball managers.	**Pages 14-15** View stars of the sport in action.	**Key Words** Study vocabulary, and play a matching word game.
Pages 16-17 Complete this mapping activity.	**Pages 18-19** Find out more about where baseball games take place.	**Pages 20-21** Watch a video about baseball players.	**Slide Show** View images and captions, and try a writing activity.
			AV² Quiz Take this quiz to test your knowledge